Photo by courtesy of the Australian Tourist Commission

D1346399

£4.25

CONT

Written and edited by Clive Hopwood
with contributions from Kate Bryson, Jean Hawkes, Pamela Hutchins,
Mike Kidson, Roy Lakeman, Bruce McMichael, Kirsty Nunn,
John Smallwood and Valerie Wooding

Designed by Ian Gwilt

Picture Credits
Australian Tourist Commission
pages 2-3,18-19, 32-33,54-55,62-63
Colorsport page 58
London Features International Ltd.
pages 6,10,13,23,26,27,31,37,42,46,56
Scope Features pages 7,17,20,21,22,23,28,40,41,50,59,61
Syndication International (1986) Ltd.
pages 14,15,20,22,24,41,45,52,53,58
Topham Picture Library pages 4,8,12,30,34,39,44,47
World Press Network Ltd. pages 4,5,9,10,11,16,36,38,57

Cover photos by Scope Features, Syndication International (1986)
Ltd. and London Features International Ltd.

World

ENTS

G'day Neighbours

Welcome to World International's third **Neighbours** book. The flagship of Australian soaps stays firmly at the top with the greatest number of weekly viewers. Since last year it has gained over a million new daily viewers.

Latest Aussie arrival *Home and Away* has made an impressive start, climbing straight into Number 4 position in the soap league, with an audience now beginning to climb over the 14 million mark – still a good 5 million plus behind good old **Neighbours**, mind you!

The late eighties British love affair with things Australian looks set to continue in increasing measure into the nineties. With Australian films and film stars, Australian pop singers, and Australian TV mini-series all making inroads into popular western culture, **Neighbours**, *Home and Away*, and their soap stablemates, are the foretaste of what is yet to come.

The invasion of the Aussies, with their amber nectar, barbies, blues, and Bondi beach, began with the likes of Mel Gibson, Barry Humphries, Paul Hogan and others. The pioneer soaps *The Sullivans*, *The Young Doctors*, and *Sons and Daughters* paved the way. **Neighbours** hit the jackpot. *Prisoner: Cell Block H, The Flying Doctors* and *Home and Away* have all reaped the rewards of Australian popularity . . . often with the same actors.

Maybe it's all that sunshine and greenery, just like Anne Charleston says, or maybe it's a desire for a fresh approach, a change from the glossy fantasy of the American supersoaps and the gritty realism of the home-grown British soaps. Whatever it is, the Poms are certainly hooked on **Neighbours**!

The Australian success story has only just begun.

1990 LOGIE AWARDS
Most Popular Drama
NEIGHBOURS
Best Actor
CRAIG McLACHLAN
Best Actress
RACHEL FRIEND

Meet the Ramsays

Neighbours traces the lives and loves of a group of families who live in Ramsay Street, in suburban Melbourne. We take a lighthearted look at some of the street's more famous residents, past and present . . .

MADGE changes her name a lot. To begin with she was, of course, Madge RAMSAY until she married Fred MITCHELL. After the divorce she resorted to RAMSAY again, before marrying Harold BISHOP. Rough but with a heart of gold, loud but likeable, Madge has been called 'the spirit of Australia'. No wonder she won the *Australian Mum of the Year Award*.

CHARLENE has a lot of her mother's fire, but has so far only managed MITCHELL and ROBINSON in her list of surnames. A tomboy with a tendency for trouble, she punches hard and mends cars, and was last heard of in Brisbane. Marriage to boy next door Scott has not been a bed of gladioli so far. Is there a name change in the air already?

HENRY is the joker in the family, a loveable rogue. He's been to jail once, but we all know he's a good guy really, and that his madcap schemes never truly harm anyone. Henry was the handsome hunk romantically linked with most of the available females in the street, with the possible exception of Bouncer the dog.

SHANE, the hunk before Henry, and nephew to Madge, was a champion diver until an accident spoiled his career. Always romantically involved with someone, often attracting trouble (as only the Ramsays can), he rode off into the sunset with his motorbike and most recent girlfriend. He is one of the few RAMSAYS to possess only the one surname.

And then of course there's Edna and Dan, Max, Tom, Maria, Doreen, Danny and who knows how many other unknown relations yet to be discovered as the story continues . . .

and the Robinsons

The other big name in the street, and usually outnumbering the Ramsays by about 3:2 in terms of current residents are **THE ROBINSONS**. Definitely a more stable and civilized family and household, they lack the warm rough and tumble of the Ramsays.

JIM, the father, is the anchorman of the street, the one fixed point in a changing universe. He is the elder statesman, a sensitive father, a genial pillar of the community. Sensibly married to a doctor – a wise move for any soap character.

PAUL, his son, has flashes of the ruthless speculator and cold businessman about him, but behind that smart suit and an office the size of a large cupboard lie the vulnerable emotions of a powerful man who needs to be loved. Not the kind of villain who would sell his own grandmother. This is just as well.

HELEN DANIELS is his grandmother, and lives in the same house as his dad. In Ancient Greece they had the Delphic Oracle. In Ramsay Street they have Helen Daniels, who is twice as good and only lives over the road from everybody. With a gift of diplomacy Gorbachev would envy, she knows the answer to every problem, and is almost always right.

SCOTT, the youngest son, did the time-honoured thing, and by popular demand married the girl next door, Charlene, the Ramsay fireball. He took up journalism, and carried on living at his mother's, until eventually he realized his wife now lived in Brisbane and went there, too.

And obviously we don't have time to mention Bill, Bess and James, or Anne's sister, Rosemary. Even Beverly, Jim's newest wife, and her two children, Todd and Katie – well, not hers exactly, since their name is Landers and hers was Marshall before she became a Robinson – only get a line. Jim's daughters Julie and Lucy shouldn't be forgotten in passing, nor should Paul's two wives (though not both at the same time), Terri (deceased) and Gail.

and the rest

There's even more of these than there are Ramsays and Robinsons put together. But, as is the nature of soaps, lots of them seem to have got themselves married to or divorced from one of these two families, or at the very least been romantically involved.

HAROLD BISHOP married into the Ramsays by wooing Madge. With his cuddly pomposity and well-meaning manner Harold is everyone's idea of an uncle who tries hard. A little stuffy, but full of good intentions.

DES CLARKE, the bank manager, who has large ears and specializes in being either jilted or bereaved in some way, has yet to hold on to anyone long enough to be divorced from them. Baby **JAMIE** became yet another soap single parent family and Dad eventually overcame his blues to go out looking for a new Mrs Clarke. With predictably depressing results, of course. Let's face it, Lucky is not this guy's middle name.

MRS MANGEL has moved on to pastures new with husband **JOHN WORTHINGTON**, but who could forget her? The creme de la creme of neighbourhood busybodies, she drove everyone crackers. This woman had her standards and expected everyone else to have them too. Granddaughter **JANE** evolved from Plain Jane Superbrain to cut a swathe through the street's most eligible bachelors . . . and escaped them all.

Then of course there's Nick and Joe, not forgetting Clive and Susan (who was almost a Ramsay), and Des's awful mother, Eileen, and the late, lamented Daphne the stripper. Even Bouncer the dog deserves our attention. But if we stop to look at Bronwyn, Sharon, Mike, Sue Parker, Rob Lewis, Nikki, and . . . well, Ramsay Street is a busy kind of place where people come and go, lives change, a never-ending story of friends and neighbours. Drop in there any day and you'll soon get to know who everyone is.

CHECKING OUT

Fair hair, blue eyes and cheeky ways — they were Craig McLachlan's passport to fame, even if it did mean that his wife, Karen, had to keep quiet about their marriage. It wasn't the only sacrifice she made in the end.

Craig's never been shy, that's for certain. He can talk under water with a pork sausage in his mouth, as they say in Australia, especially when it comes to talking about himself. The one time he did keep his mouth shut was when he was discussing his role of Henry with the **Neighbours** producers. He omitted to say he was married. But after two months in the part he came clean and revealed his wife, Karen.

"I'm glad the truth came out," says Craig. "I kept quiet about Karen at first, because she's very shy. And I'd already lost one acting job because I had a wife, so I was in no real hurry to tell the **Neighbours** team. When I owned up they were a bit put out — I suppose they would have preferred the image of an unattached, young bloke."

9

His agent at the time, Lela King, says, "The deception got too much of a burden for him. The poor lad could never go anywhere in public with Karen, could never talk about her, and she, for her part, had to be secretive about him."

It was Karen who did all the groundwork for Craig's next career move — a break into the music business. Craig had already had one unsuccessful band called the Y-Fronts. This was followed by Next Door, the band he formed with fellow actors Guy Pearce and Paul Keane, and after that came Good Question. Nothing happened.

Although Craig and Karen separated in 1988, she continued to manage Craig's business affairs, and it was she who finally succeeded in helping Craig to land a recording contract for the new band, Check 1-2. In November 1989 the first single, *Amanda*, was released.

"We don't ever regret being married"

"We've had a great reaction," said Craig. "The record contract with CBS is just great. Apart from the deal with me and my band, it also includes an option for nine albums, which is wonderful. It's a tremendous vehicle for my songwriting. It'll open doors for me."

But as one door opened another one closed: in this case, on Craig and Karen's marriage. Four years after their marriage, Craig began divorce proceedings. It was the beginning of the end for yet another showbiz marriage that cracked under the strain.

Craig met Karen in Bateau Bay, New South Wales, when they had lead roles in their school musical in the early 1980s. He was just 15 and she was a year older. It was a difficult time for Craig.

"My father had just died of cancer," Craig recalls. "In the eyes of a youngster it seemed unfair that Dad had died. He was a really lovely man and he died. Yet there were so many nasty pieces of work, who gave their families a hard time, still alive. I created havoc, staying up all night, getting into places when I was under age, and drinking. I advise young people to steer well clear of drink." It was Karen who helped him pull through.

When he left school he headed straight for Sydney. His good looks succeeded in

The pressures of work, coupled with the problems of coping with such adulation proved too much for their marriage and a separation was agreed. But when Karen discovered Craig's intimate friendship with Rachel Friend (Bronwyn in **Neighbours**), she realized there was no turning back.

Craig started divorce proceedings. "Karen just cracked under the pressure of serving an international heart-throb. It's tough talking about this in public, but because of my position I feel I have to. I'm not like the average Joe Blow who gets separated."

Karen says, with a trace of sadness in her voice, "We don't ever regret being married. We just knew it was time to move on. It was a fantastic marriage in every way. The only thing that destroyed it was **Neighbours**."

What destroyed their marriage ironically made Craig's career. And there too the parting of the ways have come. Although Henry's exit from the cast of **Neighbours** is still well in the future, Craig himself won't be absent from British TV screens — his debut as teacher Grant Mitchell in the rival soap *Home and Away* will make sure of that. And Check 1-2 look all set to make Craig a pop star as well. Thanks to Karen.

"The record contract is just great"

landing him some modelling work, but the pressure was too great. "I was completely blown away by the big city," he says. "I was too naive to cope with it, so I scurried back up the coast and worked as a plumber's mate and a brickie."

He tried again to break into showbusiness, but this time Karen accompanied him to Sydney to give him the moral and financial support he needed. Karen took a job as a medical secretary to pay the bills, since Craig was making no money at all.

His first break was in *The Young Doctors*, and this was followed by the part of Michael in *Sons and Daughters*, by which time Craig and Karen were married. Then came **Neighbours**, and an almost instant launch into superstardom.

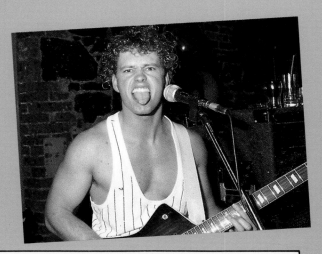

"The unearthed family tree is nothing less than a substitute village, an episode of **Neighbours** that has no limits in time and space."

Christina Hardyment
The Guardian

Paul Keane once played Romeo in Shakespeare's classic tragedy, which may seem a million miles away from the hapless Des. But Paul loves acting challenges, which for someone who appeared in *Sons and Daughters* is probably necessary. Unlike bank manager Des, Paul admits to being absolutely hopeless when it comes to money. But as a bachelor he had to practise on his sister's young son, Patrick, to prepare himself for his role as a single parent in **Neighbours**. Bet Jamie was mighty pleased that his screen dad had learned which way was up!

Neighbours is making people leave the country. That's not as bad as it sounds, for figures released by the UK Office of Population Censuses and Surveys revealed that Australia has leapt ahead of the United States as the chosen destination for people emigrating from the UK, and second only to the EEC. While *émigrés* to Canada and New Zealand fell in 1987 and 1988, Australia's share rose to 44,100, twice the number in 1985. *The Times* noted that the rise had coincided with the start of "the popular antipodean soap opera" — **Neighbours** to you and me.

The Kristiansen family from Cardiff waded through a year of Aussie immigration red tape to take their chance Down Under. "The children are all for it," said Mum. "They think they are going to live on Ramsay Street with a swimming pool in the garden!"

Would-be *émigrés* should think hard before they take the plunge, however, as recent migrant Ian Gale warns in his new book, *Successful Migration to Australia*.

Charlene and Scott may no longer be centre stage in the successful soap, but their love story lingers on. Virgin's video, *The Scott and Charlene Love Story*, shot straight into the video sales charts at number 7, and climbed right to the top. Anyone out there clammering for *Madge and Harold: the Magic Moments* or *The Nell Mangel Marriage*?

Live long and prosper. Ethel Codling, who celebrated her 104th birthday earlier this year, had some sound advice for anyone planning to live for a century: "Do not sit glued to the television." Ethel, from Nottingham, doesn't quite rule out everything. "Be selective," she advises. "Stick to *Coronation Street*, **Neighbours** and the tea-time news."

NEIGHBOURS NEWS

Plucky teenager, Olivia Murray, decided she'd make the ultimate sacrifice and not watch her favourite soap, **Neighbours**, for the best of reasons. Olivia, who is from Fulford Comprehensive School in York, fasted from televison for a week to raise money to send food for the needy people in Romania. "Friends at school teased me about it," she said, but kindhearted Olivia stuck to it, and managed to send two food parcels with the proceeds from her week without the box.

One Briton will most definitely be taking up residence in Ramsay Street: he's street wise West Indian, Eddy Buckingham. He's played by Romford born actor Bob La Castra. "Eddy's bright and breezy, and a one for chatting up the ladies," reveals Bob. "He has the gift of the gab but is an all-round nice guy. I don't think the English will find it hard to accept. After all, you have West Indian Poms on every street."

Bob emigrated to Australia with his wife, Lindsay, nine years ago. His big break came as Aussie TV's first black presenter, fronting a children's pro-gramme in 1984. His introduction into **Neighbours** will be seen during Madge and Harold's visit to England, when they invite him to Australia. "I think the fact I am English was a deciding factor," says Bob. "It'll be a great draw card for the English audience. And the producers wanted someone who was a bit of fun." We look forward to his debut.

MOVING UP

Jessica Muschamp Sharon

Jessica Muschamp is looking for an eligible young man. "I want to get married young," she says. "I know I'm only 19 but I don't intend waiting ages to have babies." While she may be in a hurry she still wants to be able to pick the best. "I'll know when the time is right, and when I've found the perfect man I won't hesitate."

There is likely to be no shortage of volunteers. Jessica has become a big hit in **Neighbours**, which she joined in May 1988. She caught the acting bug very early.

Her first stage success was at the age of three. "My sister was in an end of the year ballet," she recalls. "I was in the audience, in my tutu, but got free of my dad's grip. I got on stage and they couldn't tear me off. I remember thinking all the applause was for me."

Jessica explains, "I've always wanted to be an actress since I can remember. You only get one sort of life — an air hostess, a farmer, a vet — but with acting you can be them all!" But being Sharon can sometimes be inhibiting when it comes to meeting and going out with men.

"It's not that the rehearsals and filming take up my time, but more a matter of feeling confident with people, especially boys or men that I meet. It's a tough situation because it's difficult to know who to trust."

Being a soap star obviously has its

actresses and there's no envy at all; they're really pleased for me."

Just to show there is no side with Jessica, she visited England in the summer to be a bridesmaid at her pen pal Jackie's wedding. The two long distance friends met for the first time last Christmas, and got on really well. There was no doubting the recognition by Jessica's English fans either. "When we went shopping she kept on being stopped for her autograph," says Jackie. "People couldn't believe it was her. She handled it really well."

"I want to get married young"

drawbacks. Jessica gives an example: "I might be at a club or wherever and be approached by a man who starts talking to me. I think, 'Well, that's nice,' and then he starts talking to me as Sharon and everything falls flat. I know then that he's approached me because of what I'm well known for rather than for the person I really am."

Coping with stardom means socializing with friends. "I need to keep in contact with ordinary people just to keep normal," says Jessica. "If I didn't I'd go crazy. I might be ambitious as an actress but not to the exclusion of everything else in my life. Fortunately I've kept a lot of my friends from before I started **Neighbours**. A couple are

"It's difficult to know who to trust"

"Parents and young people will say this is the highlight of their day to watch **Neighbours**. It's because it depicts the whole family and it always tends to go through all the dramas and irritations of everyday life, but yet in the end, when it comes to a crisis, they will come together, not only just in the family but in the neighbourhood situation."

Valerie Riches
Family & Youth Concern

career. The studios are only an hour's drive from her family's 10 acre spread where she lives with her parents. Dad is a philosophy lecturer and Mum teaches in a primary school. They all enjoy a free and easy lifestyle among a collection of horses, dogs and cats, Jessica's Welsh pony, chickens (for free range eggs), and sheep (for their wool).

Jessica gets on very well with her older sister, Miranda, and older brother, Guy. "Although I am much younger I never felt left out," she says. "I was just the little sister and they used to take me everywhere with them. The gap's closed now, and Miranda and I go out shopping like sisters do, and confide in each other. But I could never pinch her make-up because she doesn't wear any! It's different with clothes and as soon as I got to her size I was forever dipping into her wardrobe."

"I didn't expect to get the part"

Jessica has already had some practice at handling difficult situations. She managed to combine working on **Neighbours** with finishing her Higher School Certificate. She had intended devoting that year entirely to study, even missing out on the school play. "When the **Neighbours** audition came up I thought it would be good experience, but I didn't expect to get the part of Sharon. Then when I did I had some serious thinking to do."

In the end she opted to both work and study – and passed her HSC with flying colours! "I seriously think that doing **Neighbours** was what got me through. I don't think I would have finished the year if I hadn't had anything else but school to think about."

With her success in the soap Jessica is now concentrating her efforts on her acting

In fact, away from the cameras Jessica likes to slop around in a comfortable old track suit. She is also a dedicated vegetarian. "I was 13 when I decided to become one. The family all decided at the same time and we have never looked back."

Jessica insists she is a world apart from Sharon, the impetuous, laid back character in **Neighbours**. "Sharon comes from a dusty, isolated town and wants to come to the bright lights of the city," Jessica explains. "I like her character. She's a bubbly person, but she is tactless. She doesn't mean to insult people but she's thoughtless. She has a lot of boyfriends, more than me! – a different one every week."

Which is where we came in. Jessica still dreams of that handsome knight in shining armour who will one day whisk her off to marital bliss. Until then she says she intends staying at home with Mum and Dad. "At 19 I don't think I should start worrying yet about being left on the shelf."

"Can there be a tree left standing in the entire Australasian continent, as so many of them seem to have been felled to provide *actors* for the soaps?"

Paul Stevens
Bristol Evening Post

THE WONDERFUL WIZARDS OF OZ

Rupert Murdoch

The *Dirty Digger*, as the middle-aged enfant terrible of newspaper publishing is popularly known, was born in Melbourne in 1931. He was educated locally at first, then at Oxford, where it is said he had a reputation as a liberal and kept a small bust of Lenin in his study!

Murdoch began his publishing career in 1952, when he inherited the ownership of the *Adelaide News* from his father. In the years following he built up the empire now known as The News Corporation. He now controls two Australian commercial television stations and publishes Australia's only national newspaper.

He first came to the attention of the British public in 1968, when he acquired the *Sun*, which he turned into a wildly successful and controversial tabloid. Its emphasis on sensational journalism has influenced many other newspapers. Since then he has extended his holdings to include the equally sensational *News of the World* and, since 1982, the more traditional *Times* and *Sunday Times*.

More recently Murdoch has collaborated with Alan Sugar, owner of the Amstrad electronics firm, to develop the Sky satellite broadcasting network. His approach to news reporting has already made an indelible mark on British society: through his interest in new broadcasting technology it will undoubtedly continue to do so.

Barry Humphries

A multi-talented actor and writer, Barry Humphries eventually became a star – but at the cost of his own identity . . .

Born in Melbourne in 1934, and educated at the local grammar school and university, Barry began his career as a repertory actor at Melbourne's Union Theatre. In the late 1950s he moved to England, appearing in *Demon Barber* and then creating the role of Sowerberry in *Oliver!*

Rather than continuing in a straightforward acting career, Barry staged a succession of one-man shows during the 1960s. At the same time he regularly contributed poems and a comic strip (*The Adventures of Barry McKenzie*) to the satirical magazine *Private Eye*.

It was in the mid-1970s that Barry achieved lasting success when he developed the outrageous persona of Dame Edna Everage, Australia's gladioli-wielding, self-styled, unofficial cultural ambassador. Edna's extraordinary rise to fame has eclipsed Barry's own reputation, and has gone far beyond his original aim of poking fun at British perceptions of Australian culture. Her larger-than-life character has become familiar to millions through appearances such as hosting a section of Comic Relief.

Meanwhile Barry appears content to bask in her shadow, happily pursuing his stated hobby of "reinventing Australia"!

The heart of the Australian continent is desert. The cities cluster along the more fertile coasts, and beyond the city limits lies the bush. But travel directly inland from any point on the coast and you will, before long, hit desert that stretches for thousands of miles. This is the outback.

It comprises three quarters of this vast, ancient continent. It contains some of the most breathtaking landscapes on the planet. A place of intense isolation, where people may go for months without seeing others, it is a world where nature is supreme, and man only a visitor.

THE NEVER NEVER

It is also a world of mystery, the 'Never Never' or 'sunset country', a place where the giant beings of the world's dawn lie sleeping underground, or formed into fantastic rock structures.

The modern world seems very distant, the skylines of the 20th century out of sight, out of mind. Before you is an ancient landscape, majestic in its sheer scale, profound with its own history, to which humanity is a comparative newcomer.

A hundred years ago Ernest Giles crossed the Gibson Desert, partly on foot, and named it after his companion, Alfred Gibson, who had died with his horse somewhere in a thousand miles of scorched emptiness. With temperatures between 40°C (104°F) by day and -10°C (14°F) by night, Giles described the place as 'hell on earth'.

AN UNTAMED LAND

Nowadays with highways — often little more than rutted tracks — crossing this last frontier, it is possible to explore the outback in more safety than Gibson. Nevertheless, a four-wheel drive vehicle and a two-way radio are essentials.

The outback is an untamed land, a state of mind as much as it is a place. Nowhere else in the world will you experience such a true sense of mankind's tiny role in a vast universe.

ALIAN EXPERIENCE

The Outback

courtesy of the Australian Tourist Commission

19

SOAP

Sixty years

Half a century has passed since the phenomenal genre of soap operas first burst upon an unsuspecting public. Since they began, the lives and loves, the triumphs and disasters of thousands of soap opera characters have captivated the hearts of millions of addicted followers. But how did they begin, and why do we love them so much?

The next time you wash your face, look in the mirror, for it's people just like you (providing, that is, that you wash!) who brought about the birth of the long-running daily dramas. Back in the 1920s broadcasting was in its infancy. While Britain chose to pay for the new radio service through a licence fee, in America it was commercial radio that won the day.

As well as running straight advertisements the Americans elected to exploit commercial sponsorship. This meant that a company wishing to reach a large audience with its product would pay for a programme to be made and broadcast. Clearly, the more popular a programme the more people would hear about the product.

The race was well and truly on to come up with a winning formula. By the late 1920s America had a nationwide broadcasting system, and radio had been joined by a growing television industry. The audiences could be measured in millions.

Among the biggest sponsors of the day were the large soap producing companies, like Colgate-Palmolive and Proctor and Gamble. Their target audience was the American housewife, and their answer was the daily drama with its identifiable characters and storylines, and the all-important cliffhanger which kept fans hooked for the next episode . . . and, of course, the next plug for the product.

Soap companies were the major sponsors of these continuing stories, and so the term 'soap opera' was born. Nobody knows who coined the phrase, nor for that matter why 'opera', since these dramas were spoken not sung. But soap opera stuck, even though neither soap nor opera has anything to do with such descendants as **Neighbours**, *Crossroads* or *Coronation Street*.

THE FIRST SOAPS

Ironically it was not soap but toothpaste that spawned the very first serial, *Amos and Andy*, on a Chicago local radio station. A comedy revolving around two black characters (played, bizarrely, by two white actors), it soon went national six days a week, attracting an audience of 40 million.

The move from comedy to drama, and closer to today's concept of a soap, was the inspiration of Chicago schoolteacher Irna Phillips. She came up with *Painted Dreams*, which although it never attracted a major sponsor and was short-lived, gave Irna the opportunity to explore and develop many of the standard ingredients of the soap style.

Today's Children was her first big hit, a drama centred on the ups and downs of family life – the central core of virtually every successful soap opera since. Although others have added to and elaborated on Irna's pioneering work, most of the basic characteristics of soap were invented by her. Her greatest success, *The Guiding Light*, is – believe it or not – still running on American television to this day.

The other major contributors to soap opera as we know it were a husband and wife team, Frank and Anne Hummer, who worked in local radio in – you've guessed it – Chicago. They widened out the scope of the stories, making them more sensational, and introducing a pronounced degree of melodrama into the family life of soap characters. Their story, *Bob and Betty*, became the very first nationally broadcast soap in America.

ENTER THE ROBINSONS

The first British soap was, by a quirk of fate, first heard in America. The quirk was the Second World War, and *Front Line Family* was broadcast by the BBC on their North American Service.

The Robinson family epitomised, for propaganda purposes at least, the plucky British family facing up to Hitler in the still dark days of 1942. Their popularity spread when the BBC Overseas Service took the show, and soon British listeners were demanding the right to hear their own soap.

Subsequently it was broadcast in the UK under the title *The Robinsons*. It remained Britain's only soap for six years, until it was superseded by *Mrs Dale's Diary*. This proved a big hit and ran continuously until 1969.

The real classic British radio soap, still very much with us, didn't arrive on the scene until 1950. This was *The Archers*, originally designed not to sell soap but to help boost Britain's post-war food production, with useful information on

farming wrapped around a story of everyday country folk.

Radio soaps dominated the scene on both sides of the Atlantic, but television's boom in the 1950s soon began to claw away the audiences, and the heyday of radio soaps was gone.

The likes of *Waggoner's Walk* and more recently *Citizens* have been but minor dots on the landscape. In America the demise of the radio soap came even earlier. TV soap had arrived to stay.

TV SOAP: THE EARLY DAYS

A Woman to Remember was the first televised soap in 1947, but it was Proctor and Gamble's *The First Hundred Years* in 1950 that really got the genre going. Showing on CBS it soon gained a popular following, and NBC responded with *Hawkins Falls*. The TV soap wars began with a vengeance.

The pattern of daytime and evening soaps originated in the USA. Daytime soaps were more cheaply produced, and always studio-bound due to the limited budget. Often under-rehearsed and performed live, they were the bottom line so far as soap quality went. They were broadcast throughout the week.

Big money, location work, and more famous stars became the hallmark of the flashier evening soaps. Better in quality all round, these were broadcast once or twice weekly at most. The gradual switch over to video did, however, herald an all-round improvement, considerably reducing on-screen mistakes.

In Britain the launch of ITV brought new competition to the BBC. The soap gauntlet was thrown down in 1960 with the first episode of *Coronation Street*, although the BBC's *The Grove Family* and ATV's *Emergency – Ward Ten* from the mid-1950s were the forerunners of British TV soap.

Coronation Street, however, was in a class of its own, often transcending soap standards with top quality scripts and high production values. It rapidly gathered a massive popular audience. BBC's *Compact*, set around a magazine, *United*, based on a football club, and *The Newcomers*, about life in a new town, all failed to make any impact on the ITV flagship.

What may go down in history as the worst TV soap in British broadcasting managed to run for a staggering 24 years. The late lamented *Crossroads* managed to be both a national laughing stock and immensely successful at the same time.

THE NEW GENERATION

In America really big bucks began to fuel a new brand of soap operas which boasted 35mm film (just like movies) and even the movie stars to match.

Dallas (1978) and *Dynasty* (1981) started a ratings war such as the soaps had never seen, with more and yet more money being thrown into the battle. They took America by storm, and went on to conquer Britain shortly afterwards. Unlike the daily soaps, running continuously throughout the year, these supersoaps were given the classy showcases reserved for top quality drama series – prime-time evening slots, once weekly, and for limited seasons only.

In Britain today's present stable of soaps began to line up. *Crossroads* finally died in 1988, despite public outcry. Taking its place came *Emmerdale*, Channel 4's *Brookside*, and in 1985 the BBC finally came up with a real winner in *EastEnders*.

It soon overhauled *Coronation Street*, for so long the only horse in a one-horse race. Competition from *Dallas* and *Dynasty*, followed by their less remarkable offspring, *Knots Landing*, *The Colbys* and *Falcon Crest*, suddenly made British TV seem awash in soap. 'You ain't seen nothing yet' would have been an appropriate prediction at that time.

The real revolution was still to come. And it came not from the USA or Britain, but Australia. With the advent of daytime television for the first time in Britain, cheap programming was suddenly at a very high premium – soaps, along with game shows and studio chats, proved to be the answer, and Australia had soaps-a-plenty to spare.

Neighbours has totally changed the face of British soap. Since its arrival with a five days a week, twice-daily screening pattern, both *EastEnders* and *Coronation Stre*et have been forced to get their acts together. Extra episodes and repeat screenings, and the need for even better scripts have brought British soap opera to its peak.

Legions of other Aussie soaps have attracted new audiences in the wake of the **Neighbours** success, *Home and Away* being one of the latest – but no means the last – import from Down Under.

Between them the Aussie soaps now command a bigger total audience than either their British or American rivals in this country. And it's all thanks to someone who wanted people to wash their hands with their company's brand of soap.

Someone's cleaning up, that's for sure.

LOVEABLE AND HONEST

Ian Smith *Harold*

Meat-eating, scotch-drinking Ian Smith is nothing like the stuffy character he plays in Neighbours. He shares the same cuddly shape, is as loveable and honest as dear old Harold, but the real Ian is a lot more fun.

'Overnight' success in show business after thirty years can be a bit frightening, however. "There seems to be a worldwide Harold Bishop fan club," says Ian, obviously amazed that such a thing could exist. "I get mobbed everywhere, and I can't even go to the shops without signing autographs. It's incredible and I must admit I've been really scared."

Ian also writes scripts for **Neighbours**. In fact, it was scriptwriting that led to his role as Harold Bishop in the first place. When he went to deliver his first script they asked him to audition for the new part of Harold, and he got it. The director let him develop the part as he saw it.

He may be an awful stick-in-the-mud at times, but it's hard not to find a soft spot for the well-meaning Harold. Not that he hasn't drawn a few outraged comments in his time. Scouters felt that he demeaned the authority of a Scoutmaster with his old-fashioned, jolly approach to Scouting. A vicar in Lancashire wondered who could possibly want to be a Christian if dear old Harold was an example of one!

"I've had a great time," says Ian. "I think Harold is popular because he has gumption, and if he feels he is right he will say so and

He progressed from there to earning his living as a commercial traveller. "I was one of those people they are always making jokes about. I didn't like it at all," he recalls. "I eventually lost the job, and decided to study operatic singing, which I did for six years."

"I get mobbed everywhere"

carry on regardless. People will agree with 70 per cent of what he says . . . he's a loveable character, totally honest." The gentle humour that Ian brings to the role is undoubtedly a contributory factor to Harold's popularity, which prevents his occasional pomposity from becoming too objectionable.

Ian eventually successfully auditioned for his first professional stage show, *The Desert Song*, and it put the theatre into his blood. A Gilbert and Sullivan season followed, and then, just before playing the lead in *Fiddler on the Roof*, he toured New Zealand as a honeymoon with his wife, Gail.

"Singing in **Neighbours** is difficult because I have to make it sound as if I can't sing," says Ian. "If you've had the proper training, the technique keeps popping up."

Ian and Gail have no children. "It wasn't smart for actors to have kids," explains Ian, "because you never knew when you'd be

"I've had a great time"

Ian writes a lot of the **Neighbours** scripts, but never anything for his own character. "If I came up with something particularly good for him, the other actors could accuse me of favouritism. It is a good show to write for. It's popular because it doesn't try to be superior to the viewers."

Called 'The Professor' at school, because of his plumpness and glasses, Ian left at fourteen and went to work in a warehouse.

working. It was such an insecure job." They enjoy life as a couple very much, however, and are comfortable in their home in Elsternwick. Ian and Gail are very active in the local community.

"We're great friends with the neighbours," says Ian. "They're nothing like that lot in Ramsay Street . . . thank goodness!"

"I first got the idea for **Neighbours** in England watching *Coronation Street*. I spent long enough in England to know that **Neighbours** was just right for viewers over there too."

Reg Watson
creator of **Neighbours**

Kristian Schmid, one of **Neighbours** youngest stars, is getting used to the adulation, but it hasn't been easy. "Sometimes I think being a kid is harder than being an adult," he says, especially when he has to do his schoolwork on top of being a soap star. Girl fans are just one of the problems attached to being a 14-year-old celebrity. "Girls of 13 and 14 write to me," he smiles. "They want to know all kinds of things. Girls are always recognizing me and coming up to confront me. I don't mind, but sometimes it can be very difficult if I'm with a girl I really like." Kristian's busy work schedule keeps him apart from his family in Geelong, so he stays with some relatives in Melbourne for up to four days at a time. "It can get pretty tiring," says handsome Kristian. Life can certainly be tough at 14.

Live court hearings could rival the ratings of soaps like **Neighbours**, *Coronation Street* and *EastEnders*, claim the Bar Council. Seeking amendments to the Broadcasting Bill in parliament, they cited the case of America, where the courts are tele-vised in over 40 states, bringing the dirty laundry of celebrated civil and criminal hearings into the front rooms of millions. Sounds great, if they could only find a way of televising them with lots of outdoor sunshine, good looking lawyers in their teens, and a catchy theme tune.

Linda Hartley, who plays Harold's only daughter Kerry Bishop, had a battle on her hands in real life just when she was beginning to make it in **Neighbours**. An anorexia sufferer in her teens, Linda recovered, but still found her health was dogged by problems. Co-star Mark Little (Joe Mangel) advised her to see a naturo-path specializing in food allergies. It turned out that Linda was prey to the yeast infection, *candida*. Now she's on a diet of green vegetables, certain grains and fruits, buckwheat, and bread that contains neither yeast nor wheat — and she is now as fit as a fiddle at last!

One of Britain's most outspoken and controversial TV presenters has finally come clean about what turns him and his television on: the soaps. "It's a terrible embarrassment," con-fesses James Whale, best known for his rude and abrasive manner on his infamous phone-in TV show, "but I shall continue to watch them, even if it's bad for my credibility. I know everything there is to know about British soap operas but I have never seen an American one. I've watched **Neighbours** for years — I love it and if I don't manage to see it live I have it recorded."

NEIGHBOURS NEWS

Pupils who go to orthodox Jewish schools could be expelled for watching **Neighbours**. Television soaps are definitely not on the curriculum here. Television glamorizes the breaking of commandments, and runs counter to the ethos of Jewish religious schools.

Everything depends on your point of view of course. Young Conservative activist Graham Robb feels that, "The popularity of **Neighbours** shows that the British public want to see programmes which, although presenting the ups and downs of life, do show families in a positive light."

Soap aficionados were given the treat of a lifetime at the BHP Television Festival in Perth last February. Early episodes from no less than 36 soap series were screened for their pleasure, including our very own *Coronation Street*, as well as Aussie favourites *Possession, Punishment* and the classic *Number 96*. The real fireworks and passion were left until the end of the festival when they debated the motion, 'Soap is the Religion of Our Time'!

Fiona Corke has become another statistic in the list of stars who have now left the cast of **Neighbours** in Australia. 1989 proved a bad year for the soap's producers since, having already lost Kylie Minogue and Jason Donovan, they were faced with an exodus that included firm favourites Annie Jones, Guy Pearce, Craig McLachlan, Rachel Friend and Mark Scott-Stevens, as well as Anne Scott-Pendlebury. British fans can at least comfort themselves with the thought that many of these defections are still well in the future, and for fans of Gail, in particular, you can rest assured that amongst all the ups and downs she still has to face with Paul there is at least one moment of pure joy to come for her.

TOUGH LOVE

Anne Charleston Madge

There's a lot of real life experience in Anne Charleston's portrayal of Madge Bishop. As a working single parent, Anne's own background has proved to be the foundation of Madge's character, particularly when it comes to being mum to the Ramsay clan.

To her children Madge dispensed what Anne calls 'tough love' – love and discipline, which viewers seemed to appreciate. Younger ones began to write to ask if she could please adopt them. Older ones voted her Australian TV's *Mum of the Year*.

Anne herself is a third-generation Australian. Her great-grandparents on both sides emigrated from Ireland in 1860 and settled in Victoria. When Anne was born in the early 1940s her brother Peter, then ten, was not impressed by the new arrival — especially since she was a girl. As a result she became a somewhat shy, lonely girl. But even as a child of five or six, the idea was forming in her mind that she would be an actress when she grew up.

"According to my mother I was an absolutely vile girl, quite off-putting really," laughs Anne. "She thought my speech was so bad that nobody would understand me. My mind was working faster than my mouth — I gabbled." Fortunately for Anne's future career her mother took her for elocution lessons.

To Anne this was a terrific break: it was the first step to becoming an actress. The family were not so sure about that. "We were pretty basic middle class," says Anne.

"I found life difficult as a single mum"

"Both my father and mother wanted me to become a secretary and marry the boss. That was the fate of most girls at the time, but I was a bit of a rebel, and I became responsible for most of my mother's grey hairs!"

With typical Madge-like determination Anne set out to achieve her ambition, receiving her mother's acquiescence if not her blessing. "All right," exclaimed her mother, "*be* an actress!"

"I became a model during the day," recalls Anne, "and did amateur theatre at night. At first I did photographic and showroom modelling, and then gradually went into the professional theatre. In spite of my early childish talk of wanting to be an actress, my parents were horrified that any daughter of theirs wanted to go on the stage. But once I became moderately successful they bragged to all their friends!"

All was not plain sailing, however. In her first stage play, Anne brought the house down during a song-and-dance routine. She was supposed to make a graceful exit at the top of a flight of stairs. Instead she slipped and tumbled down to wild applause from an

audience who thought she was an acrobat.

When she was 26 she married actor-singer David Ravenswood. "We first met in a bar when he was appearing on stage in *Half a Sixpence* on one side of the street, and I was on stage in *Spring and Port Wine* on the other. We were married a couple of years,

but it was a total mismatch. We were just wonderful friends — and we still are. He has successfully married again and has another two children."

At 28 Anne faced the problem of having to bring up their son, Nicholas, single-handed. She worked as a barmaid, a cook, a chambermaid, anything to make ends meet between small acting jobs. "There were times when I found life difficult as a single mum," she says. "We were poor, but never seriously poor, because I could always find some sort of work to keep us going."

"I was a bit of a rebel"

A later addition to the family was Emma, Anne's cousin's daughter. "Emma's mum — a single parent — died of cancer," explains Anne. "We were like sisters, so I decided to adopt 13-year-old Emma, who wanted to come and live with me. I took Emma in because her mother's death was a huge loss, and is bound to leave emotional scars on someone her age. Poor Emma's life changed completely, and my only regret was having to work every day on **Neighbours** – I

"Unless you've done it and had to cope with the pressures you can't understand."
Darius Perkins
the first Scott Robinson

couldn't be home all the time to look after her."

With Anne as her new mother Emma got over her terrible loss. "She settled in quite quickly," says Anne, "and calls me 'Mum'. And Nicholas calls her 'Little Sis'. Just looking at her happy face has made it all worthwhile."

Family life isn't easy for soap stars, but

the shopping, which is a necessity because I'd just get mobbed in the supermarket on a Saturday. She also cleans round the house, but the kids are good and know they're expected to help out."

Clearly Anne has little spare time, but what there is she makes good use of. She's a patron of London's Great Ormond Street Children's Hospital Charity Appeal Trust, and was put in charge of Australian fund-raising. She does counselling for Aids sufferers, and tapes talking books for the blind.

Although divorced, Anne says she hasn't been put off marriage for good. "If the right man came along I'd marry him," confides Anne. "But after all this time he'd have to be very special. In fact, I've almost remarried a couple of times. A good relationship would be stunning. I'm past the age of having more children, so I don't really see the necessity of getting married. But it would depend. If I met someone who was absolutely wonderful and he wanted to get married, I might."

While **Neighbours** continues successfully there seems little chance Anne will ever find

"If the right man came along I'd marry him"

Anne makes sure it's never neglected. "I always cook dinner myself every night, and Nick and Emma help with the washing up. After the meal I like to make some attempt at communication with them before I flop into bed. Once a week I've got someone to do

the time. "We have a really killing schedule on **Neighbours**," she says. "It's like a pressure cooker! We actually film the equivalent of a feature length movie each week — and you know how long they take over those!"

And Mr Right? Anne smiles. "A man in my life would get fed up within a week." Not so her devoted fans. TV's favourite mum is fine by them.

> "It's a nice enough show, I suppose, but for the life of me I can't understand why it's done so well in Britain."
>
> *Ron Casey*
> General Manager of Channel 7, who axed **Neighbours**

SEARCH-A-WORD

Forty-seven neighbours, two television companies and a swimming pool await you in this year's fiendish Seach-a-Word. You'll find them in straight lines, but they may read forwards, backwards, up, down, or even diagonally. The list awaits . . . the search is on!

```
S H A R O N O S T A W G E R S M
H W M S I W E L B O R I A L I B
A Y I K Y L S E D A N N E T C E
N B J M A D G E E J O I C B N V
E O P I M T E R R I N H B A N E
S T I A E I I O F A E U Y E Y R
B R O N W Y N E D L H R L D R L
H I Y A C L J G L C B H E N R Y
A U S U A L I O P E N A J I E A
G L L H J A M I E O N R O C K S
A L A D O S H O H L O O K K I M
I D E N H P A D P A U L X R M A
L A N D E C L I V E E D Z A A R
L I S A N E T L E N N A H C M M
N E L L M A N G E L N C J O H N
E N E L R A H C D N A T T O C S
```

Scott and Charlene   Mitchell   Sharon   Shane   Amanda   Toby   Des
Swimming pool   Bishop   Chubb   Fiona   Daphne   Fred   Tom
Nell Mangel   Daniels   Madge   Kerry   Terri   Paul   Max
Bronwyn   Ramsay   Henry   Katie   Harold   John   Dan
Reg Watson   Beverly   Sally   Jamie   Bryan   Alan   Ian
Channel Ten   Clive   Jane   Anne   Lisa   Lucy   Joe
Rob Lewis   Mark   Edna   Nick   Guy   Gail   Len
Jim   BBC

Answers on page 61.

THE AUSTRALIAN

An iridescent wonderland of colours, the sub-marine world of corals and exotic fish, home to countless aquatic creatures, this is the Great Barrier Reef of Australia.

Stretching almost 2,000 kilometres along the coast of Queensland these crystal clear waters are one of the natural wonders of the world. The horizon seems far away across the Pacific Ocean, the warm sea a kaleidoscope of blues, ultramarines and turquoise.

FANTASTIC COLOURS

Beneath the sea's surface lies the coral reef. The reef is a living entity of large colonies of polyps, layered one on top of another, who have bound themselves together. The 300 different species provide a glorious spectrum of colours — blue, brown, pink, purple, and red.

Their beauty is mirrored by the abundance of fantastically coloured marine life, including 1,400 different species of fish. Along the northern part of the reef giant black marlin swim, and both sharks and rays make their home along the whole length of the reef.

Photos by courtesy of the Australian Tourist Commission

XPERIENCE

The Coral Reef

In truth the Great Barrier Reef is made up of two quite separate layers of reefs. One lies close to the shoreline, the other extends up to 50 kilometres out into the Pacific Ocean.

UNDERWATER DOWN UNDER

One particularly unwelcome guest in northern Queensland in the summer is the sea wasp. Also known as the box jellyfish, it carries venom which can be lethal. All beaches carry warnings against ocean swimming, although the island beaches are considered safer during this hot season.

But think of crystal clear, warm waters, white sands, spectacular marine life — best seen by glass-bottomed boat or at places like the underwater observatory on Green Island — and you have the reef. Fishing and water sports are other popular activities, as it seems mountain building.

In the city of Townsville they've been adding dirt to the top of their mightiest mound, Castle Hill, so that it can qualify officially as a mountain. Meanwhile, the Great Barrier Reef is already there.

HARD KNOCKS

Paul Keane *Des*

**Mild-mannered bank manager, Des Clarke, likes
Meatloaf and Led Zeppelin, and loves playing drums
along with his favourite heavy metal bands.
A likely story? In fact it's actor Paul Keane who
particularly likes this sound of music, although
it would be nice to think that Des was a secret
heavy metal freak – a habit that would be hard
to hide in the quiet backwater of Ramsay Street!**

Paul did get a chance to air his skills as a
drummer in public, however, when he teamed
up with **Neighbours** co-stars, Craig and
Guy, to form the short-lived rock band, Next

Door. They had hoped the band would be
their passport to the pop world, but although
this never materialized they did have fifteen
minutes of fame . . . or thirty minutes to be

precise.

The band performed before 2,000 fans at Brisbane's Festival Hall, and raised £10,000 for charity. In their half-hour session they played six songs, all written by themselves, with Paul belting out the drumbeat like a born again heavy metal missionary.

Critics and fans seemed to approve. Said

Chinese boxing for many years. He still has his strong religious roots, collects antiques, and has been writing a novel.

As unlucky Des he has to put up with more than his fair share of hard knocks. After four failed attempts at getting married he finally won Daphne for his bride, and was blessed with Jamie for a son, only to have his happiness snatched away when Daphne was killed.

"Less shy on stage than off"

one newspaper, "Paul Keane, less shy on stage than off, provided a driving beat on the drums and joined in backing vocals as the three belted out a string of home-grown songs. Verdict — Next Door brought the house down!"

Like everything Paul does he was totally committed and gave 100 per cent. He's used to having to graft hard for what he gets, a determination that doubtless has its roots in his childhood. "When I was a child we never had any money," he says.

Born the youngest of three sons and a daughter, Paul was educated at the Catholic Balmain High School in Sydney, where his interest in drama was first apparent. His initial career, however, was as a top rugby player. His successful career was only brought to an end when he smashed his collar bone.

Recovering from the devastating loss gave Paul the chance as an actor to show his sensitive playing. "It was about time Des collected his thoughts and emotions and got on with life," said Paul. "I really looked forward to working more with Annie and a change in storylines." Certainly the romance between Des and Jane gave viewers hope that luck might at last be turning in a positive direction for the unfortunate bank manager, but Annie's decision to quit **Neighbours** necessitated Des's fortunes running to form.

"It was time Des got on with life"

Even now he still maintains a strong interest in sporting activities, and is very keen on the martial arts, having studied

There can be few people who can claim to have genuinely made the general public feel sorry for a bank manager, and it's perhaps a tribute to Paul's skill as an actor that he has more than succeeded. As for other acting ambitions Paul has one in particular — he'd love to appear on ITV's *The Bill*. "It's superb," he says.

"I think in the middle of winter it's great to see all the sun. It's very popular with the kids – nine out of ten watch it. Housewives watch it as well."

Phil Tusler
The Sun

TAKING OFF

Annie Jones has taken off and is flying high, quite literally, towards new successes. The 23-year-old beauty who shot to fame as Plain Jane Superbrain in Neighbours had to take flying lessons before joining the airborne soap *Flying Doctors*, after leaving Ramsay Street in the summer of 1989.

The Aussie stunner landed the part of Lorna Jackson, and she predicts that her new role will suit her down to the ground. "My own teenage years were just like Lorna's," she says. "In the series I play an opal miner's daughter." Annie's real life dad was himself an opal miner.

Lorna is a very different character from Jane. "Jane was a real goody-goody," says Annie. "Sweet and innocent. She never smokes or drinks or swears." She adds, laughing, "She's not a bit like me. I get angry and I get mad."

However, the wide-eyed next-door charm of Jane struck a chord with her fans. Annie was swamped with letters from young girls saying how much they'd love to have her as a big sister.

In fact, Annie might never have become an actress at all. Her childhood ambition was to be an archaeologist. "I loved digging around in the dirt in places you've never heard of. I found lots of fossils which are now in museums, although I kept one particularly beautiful shell."

"Acting's a lot of hard work"

After a stint of teenage modelling — she was a magazine cover girl at the age of 14 — she was spotted by a film producer. Although she'd never had a drama lesson in her life, Annie was signed up by the South Australian Film Corporation for the film *Run Chrissie Run*. Some documentary work in Adelaide, a small part in another film, *Robbery Under Arms*, and then came the big break — a role in the original series of *The Henderson Kids*.

"It hit me then," she says, "that if I really wanted to be serious about this I'd have to move to Melbourne or Sydney to be around

"Jane's not a bit like me"

when auditions were happening. So I came to Melbourne. I worked in restaurants, boutiques and as a cocktail waitress." These paid the bills while she looked for acting jobs.

Landing a part in *Sons and Daughters* meant packing up and moving to Sydney. It was there she really caught the acting bug. "I kind of fell in love with it," she recalls. "I thought it was so glamorous. Now I realize it's a lot of hard work!"

Sheer determination got her into **Neighbours**, although she found the tag of 'the next Kylie' particularly tiresome. "I found it quite insulting," she says candidly. "There's no need for me to be the *next* anyone. I've no desire to be anything other than what I am."

As the one and only Annie Jones she was voted Australia's most popular TV actress. "I didn't expect to get the award — I was thrilled, flattered and, well, embarrassed. I'm lucky I don't get too many hassles from fans. In Kylie's shoes I'd get triple the amount. But the adrenalin keeps you going. Every day is a new challenge."

Among the biggest challenges in **Neighbours** were the on-set passionate clinches with actor Paul Keane, during Des's romance with Jane. "It's all right while you're doing it," she explains, "because you're only

> "Lorry drivers get more than soap stars in Australia."
> *Anne Haddy*

involved with what's happening to your character. But when the director calls 'cut' you stand back and realize all the crew have been watching. Then you begin to feel a little foolish."

Annie's romance on screen coincided with her real life engagement to Paul Maloney — ironically, a director of rival soap, *Home and Away*. Annie was determined her wedding was not going to be turned into a media circus. She went to enormous lengths to ensure that the only people who turned out for the celebration were family and close friends.

The service was conducted in a beautiful country garden outside Melbourne. Annie wore an off-the-shoulder gown with shawl collar, and a circlet of flowers in her hair. Actor Stefan Dennis was amongst the guests. "It was a gorgeous setting," he says, "with exotic flowers, even a waterfall. She wanted something very romantic and she will remember it forever."

Soon after her marriage Annie decided that, after three years with **Neighbours**,

"It was time to move on"

she would quit the show. "**Neighbours** helped me to grow up. Leaving was taking a chance. Many people said, 'you've got a job — why do want to leave?' But acting is certainly not like a normal job. I learnt a great deal, but it was time to move on."

She had already starred in a mini-series, *Jackaroo*, with newcomer David McGubbin, widely tipped as (yes!) the 'next' Mel Gibson. Filming in the searing heat of Western Australia, Annie had to crop her hair and learn how to ride a horse for her part as Clare Mallory, a tempestuous 17-year-old who falls in love with a part-Aboriginal stockman on her aunt's cattle station.

Husband Paul was constantly by her side during filming. "It's good having someone there who knows what is going on in your life," says Annie.

The film's director, Michael Carson, was fulsome in his praise of Annie's talents. "She's

very hard on herself. She never takes the quick solution when it comes to acting. She is certainly set to be the one who survives the soaps — and most of them don't."

Despite hitting the big time, Annie still remains a very private person, and admits she doesn't like all the fan adoration that goes with being a star. "I prefer it not to happen," she says, "especially if it's Sunday morning and I'm rushing down to the paper shop with no make-up! That's when I feel like hiding. I'm a shy person and I don't like people making a fuss."

She is adamant that her private life remains out of the newspaper gossip columns. "I don't want to over expose myself. I suppose it's good to keep people guessing," she adds with a wink.

So long as modest and talented Annie keeps appearing on our screens, both big and small, her many fans will not complain. From now on, none of us are going to mind a trip to the *Doctors* for our weekly dose of Mrs Maloney.

Know your Neighbours

Pit your wits, dredge that memory, and if all else fails take a wild guess.

Are you a **Neighbours** expert?

1 What prize did Shane win in a darts match?

2 Where did Eileen Clarke live before she arrived in Ramsay Street?

3 Whose cake had vinegar in it at the cake competition?

4 What is the name of the local newspaper?

5 Why did Des and Harold have to have the Coffee Shop redecorated?

6 Which girl did both Scott Robinson and Danny Ramsay fall for?

7 What is the name of Joe Mangel's sister, and where does she live?

8 What illness did Nikki Dennison's mum suffer from?

9 What was the name of Lucy's parrot?

10 Who was Frederick Samuel Mitchell?

11 Why did Paul threaten to sack Madge from The Waterhole?

12 Who is Bronwyn's auntie?

13 What was the song called that Mike and Scott sent to rock star Monk McCallum?

14 What subject does Mike teach?

15 Where did Dan and Edna Ramsay first meet?

16 Something attacked Mrs Mangel before her wedding — what was it?

17 Which rebel Ramsay agreed to sell their house to the Robinson Corporation?

18 Who was better than Todd at the video arcade game?

19 Why was Henry sent to jail?

20 Which **Neighbours** actor played Dr Forrest in *The Young Doctors*?

21 Which actor plays Jamie Clarke?

22 What is the name of the local vicar?

23 John Worthington met his best man at college. What were they studying?

24 What was the name of the cat who was thought to have died of salmon mousse poisoning at the Coffee Shop?

25 What was the name Clive Gibbons gave to his tours of local rubbish dumps, roundabouts and the local gasometer?

26 James Condon played art dealer Douglas Blake. Which **Neighbours** actress is he married to in real life?

Know your Neighbours

27 Why did Paul drop out of college?

28 What is the name of the headmaster of the local school?

29 What was the name of Craig's band before **Neighbours**?

30 Who sent an anonymous letter to Mrs Mangel about Mike and a nude model in Manly?

31 Why were people so upset about Rosemary Daniels' plans for the new shopping mall?

32 What do a golf ball, a clothes peg and a tape recorder have in common?

33 What was Edna Ramsay's maiden name?

34 What did Mrs Mangel lose when Len Mangel turned up?

35 Who is the only person who dares call Madge 'Maggie'?

36 Where did Des and Harold agree not to dissolve their partnership?

37 Who taught Madge how to drive?

38 Jim fell for a woman call Zoe. What was her job?

39 When was **Neighbours** first screened in Australia?

40 Whom did Charlene punch, thinking he was a mugger?

41 Which **Neighbours** actors starred in *Dick Whittington* last Christmas?

42 Which **Neighbours** actor left to join rival soap *Home and Away*?

43 Which **Neighbours** actor used to be a milkman?

44 What was RAGGS?

45 Who saved Helen Daniels' life after her stroke?

46 Harold once showed Mrs Mangel a video which displayed natives 'shaking their watusis' as she described it. What was the video called?

47 What relation is Todd Landers to Beverly Marshall?

48 How many times has Des been jilted?

49 Who lives at Number 26 Ramsay Street?

50 What colour are Craig McLachlan's eyes?

Answers on page 61.

Ned Kelly

Hero or villain, Robin Hood or Jesse James, Ned Kelly is certainly the stuff that folk legends are made of.

He was born in a slab hut just 24 miles from Melbourne. The family lived there peacefully, although his father 'Red' Kelly died when Ned was only eleven. Ned and his brother, Dan, were great horsemen, and Ned was expert at changing brands. He was first in trouble with the law at 15, sent to prison for stealing a neighbour's horse.

Released after three months in jail, Ned worked as a station hand and timber cutter until in 1877 he took up prospecting. He didn't make a strike, and times were hard. Soon he, Dan, and two mates had formed the notorious Kelly Gang.

They robbed banks wherever they went, and cancelled poor farmers' debts by burning the papers they found in the safes. They became famous outlaws, with prices on their heads. Ballads were sung about them:

> "We rob their banks
> We thin their ranks
> And ask no thanks
> For what we do."

The policemen who pursued them were, according to Kelly, "a parcel of big, ugly, fat-necked, wombat-headed, big-bellied, magpie-legged, narrow-hipped, splay-footed sons of Irish Bailiffs or English Lords."

Three of these 'officers of justice' were killed in shoot-outs with the gang. The end was nigh. Ned had a black suit of armour made up for his final stand, and he was the last member of the gang to survive.

Although he was hanged on November 11th 1888, he felt he was wrongly convicted. His last words on the scaffold at Melbourne Jail were, "Such is life."

Errol Flynn

Flynn was to say of himself, in the words of the title of one of his films, that he had been given *Too Much Too Soon*. He was born in Hobart, Tasmania on June 20th 1909. His father was a respected marine biologist.

Always in trouble, Flynn had a stormy relationship with his mother, though he later admitted that he had been "a devil in boy's clothing."

He led a colourful early life in Australia and New Guinea before coming to England to gain experience in the theatre. His move to the glamorous Hollywood of the 1930s brought him immense and instant success.

His first film, released in 1933, was called *In the Wake of the Bounty*. On his mother's side Flynn was actually descended from a mariner who had sailed on the *Bounty*.

He played uncomplicated heroes, who were on the side of right. *The Sea Hawk*, *The Adventures of Robin Hood*, *Captain Blood*, *The Adventures of Don Juan* – all used his dark, swashbuckling heroic style to great effect.

He was the romantic hero of the screen, adored by women, envied and admired by men. Off screen, however, he was less than angelic, and said to be careless and irresponsible. Scandal seemed to hover around him.

Although his star appeal fell away in the 1950s he continued making films up to his death in 1959. His autobiography, *My Wicked Ways*, tells of a screen legend who could not quite live up to the celluloid hero he portrayed.

IN LIKE FLYNN

Guy Pearce Mike

Handsome young Guy Pearce is on the threshold of movie stardom. With three films already under his belt the future is looking rosy for Ramsay Street's perennial good guy. But the roles he's landed are a far cry from teacher, Mike Young.

Guy's launch into films over the past two years has been no mean achievement. In his first screen role he plays young rock star, Paul Dysart, in the movie *Heaven Tonight*. Paul's career reflects the unfulfilled ambitions of his father, an ageing 1960s rocker, played by John Waters.

In the $3 million movie Guy has been given the chance to show his talents as a rock singer, musician and songwriter. He wrote the theme music (released as a single) and several of the movie's songs.

In the second film, *Hunting*, which tells the story of a young man who gets involved with a media mogul, Guy plays a club bouncer opposite John Savage (of *The Deer Hunter* fame).

In the latest of his movies, *Young Flynn*, the 23-year-old heart-throb plays the young Errol Flynn, in the story of the legendary swashbuckling film star before he headed for Hollywood. The story starts in Tasmania and covers his schooling in Sydney, before going on to Flynn's involvement with razor gangs,

future," he says. Fans can rest assured that Guy won't be leaving the soap for a good while yet — at least not in the UK!

The support of his family means a great deal to him. His father died when Guy was only eight, although his mother has since remarried. "Mum and I are pretty close," he says. "When Mum first started going out it was a bit hard. I tried to keep it in the background a lot, but Mum always asked me how I felt, especially when she decided to get married. Now I feel great that she has her life and everything is going so well for her."

"A great screen presence"

his part in the gold rush of the late 1920s and early 30s. The story also covers Flynn's crocodile hunting, his swindling, his affairs with islander women, a murder charge and slave trading. Not exactly Mike Young's style!

This is his biggest role to date, and the film is expected to cause a stir across America as well as Britain when it is released. Undoubtedly Boulevard Films are impressed by Guy. Producer Frank Hampson says, "I strongly believe that Guy possesses a great screen presence, charisma and enough talent to make a great impact in films on an international scale."

Fortunately Guy is level-headed and certainly doesn't think of himself as a star. "I know that when I finish in **Neighbours** I am back to where I started from. Just because I've got work now it doesn't mean I will in the

Like most mothers she wanted the best for her son. "When I started out acting I think she was worried," says Guy. "She really wanted me to go to university and study, but now I think she is quite happy. She sees that I am coping well and I consider that I am one of the luckiest people in the world."

Besides acting, Guy's other great love is music. "I love acting," he says, "and I'd never let my music interfere with **Neighbours**. But obviously in a serial like this we've got targets to meet, and there isn't always time to be creative. So getting home to the piano is really something."

Guy seems to take being famous very coolly. "But I think everyone has to admit," he grins, "that it does give you a buzz being recognized."

"I love acting"

"There are those who believe soaps to be the shining light in a godless society. There are those who claim that the scripts have all the dramatic qualities of a manual on laying bathroom tiles. But the accepted theory seems to be that soap offers a less harmful way of wasting time than drinking, eating, firing bullets into your neighbour's fence, mindlessly punting a football around the park or gazing at the real stars outside."

Peter Laud
Sunday Times, Perth

Stefan Dennis used to have a pet called Harry. (Those with a nervous disposition should stop reading at this point.) Harry, it turns out, was a spider, a very big spider. "I think spiders are really very intelligent creatures," says Stefan. "Harry was a hairy spider as big as a hand. I think spiders have a bad time of it with people killing them for no apparent reason." Stefan may have just lost himself several hundred thousand human fans, but millions of spiders are right behind you Stef!

14-year-old Jade Amenta is a lucky girl. A student at Hoppers Crossing Secondary College in Melbourne, she won the two month role of epileptic Melissa Jarratt in **Neighbours** in competition with a lot of other young hopefuls. "I didn't think I'd get it," laughs Jade, "but I'm glad I did." Cast as Todd's girlfriend, Jade had to pucker up for the part. "There's plenty of kissing," says Todd. "It was very embarrassing at first — and the cameramen gave me a hard time." No complaints from Jade you can be sure!

The man with the gorillagrams is back in Ramsay Street, and viewers will welcome the return of funster Clive Gibbons. After his exit from the soap a couple of years back, Geoff Payne went off to become the lead actor in a new series, *City Hospital*. Sadly it never made it on to the screen. Geoff got married last year to childhood sweetheart, Kath Campbell, and the couple were all set to move to Sydney to enable Geoff to appear in another series. The honeymoon was combined with the house move — and, lo and behold, the series was can-celled. "It was a bit of a hassle," grins Geoff. "The furniture had a better honeymoon than we did." No matter, back in the **Neighbours** fold, and firmly at home in Melbourne, Geoff is winning plenty of new fans as Dr Clive, and enjoying life as a newlywed.

It may come as a great surprise to 17th century playwright Ben Jonson to learn that one of his plays actually contains the theme from **Neigh-bours**. Scholars of Jonson's best known drama, *The Alchemist*, may be forgiven for failing to recall which scene contains the hummable soap hymn, but Compass Theatre Com-pany clearly have no hang-ups when it comes to updating the classics. After all, lines from Shakespeare have been known to turn up in the unlikeliest of places, so why not a bit of traffic in the other direction?

NEIGHBOURS NEWS

wo bright new stars brought in to oost **Neighbours** popularity Down Under are reckoned to be the best thing that's happened to the top soap since Scott and Charlene. Identical twins Gillian and Gayle Blakeneny are destined to provide some romance in future episodes, with Paul Robinson being one of the likely lads. They shot to fame in the unlikely sounding children's magazine programme *Wombat*, and joined the cast of **Neighbours** at the start of 1990. They play twins Caroline and Christena, and they really are identical, which causes some interesting plot twists. Gillian and Gayle are both 23 years old, 5 feet 1 inch tall, with brown eyes, dark hair and the same weight and shoe size as each other.

Harvey Becker — no relation to Boris — is one of the top national tennis coaches, and has his own theories on why Britain consistently fails to produce top international tennis players. "When you have youngsters who prefer to watch **Neighbours** than spend half an hour practising their serve it's not difficult to see where the problem lies. It's not down to lack of facilities." It's hard to see where Mr Becker gets his facts — the Australians, who also have a third of their population addicted to the soap, don't seem to have any problem producing tennis stars.

This may not be the greatest news ever, but the findings of a survey by London Weekend Television showed that **Neighbours**, whilst being by far and away the best loved show among children with a score of 70 per cent, came a poor second to . . . the commercials, which scored a resounding 87 per cent. *Home and Away* came in at number 8, with 53 per cent.

Jessica Muschamp managed to handle the tricky business of being a soap star at the same time as sitting her Higher School Certificates. And she did it in style! With Australian History 78 per cent, 18th Century History 67 per cent, French 71 per cent, she topped the bill with 87 per cent for Literature and a whopping 98 per cent for English. Not just a pretty face!

MOTHER-IN-LAW IN A MILLION?

Anne Haddy Helen

One of the main criticisms levelled at soaps is that their characters are cardboard stereotypes. But Ramsay Street has a mother-in-law who's no joke. Of that, Anne Haddy makes quite sure.

To listen to many of our less enlightened male comedians you could be forgiven for thinking that mothers-in-law were the characters we all most loved to hate. The classic, stereotype mother-in-law is an interfering, mean, possessive and domineering figure. At the hands of stand-up comedians she is also much put upon.

Neighbours offers us instead Helen Daniels, as played attractively by veteran actress Anne Haddy. She is the near-perfect mother-in-law, certainly no stereotype. After the death of Jim Robinson's wife Anne (Helen's daughter), during the birth of young Lucy, the last of Jim's four children, Helen selflessly moved in to help him bring up the family.

As Jim first came to terms with, and then

got on top of his loss, it was always Helen who was there to offer advice, support, a shoulder to cry on. Through his difficult relationship with Zoe, Paul's secretary, during the worries about Lucy's health, even as he remarried again to Beverly, Helen was there every step of the way.

Neighbours creator, Reg Watson, paid special attention to the character of Helen when he formulated the original concept of the soap. Taking as his starting point a street with the lives of three different families intertwined, he began with the Robinsons, a

"I hoped to bring out the warmth"

household of six: Jim, his children Paul, Julie, Scott and Lucy, and Helen, his mother-in-law and the children's granny.

"Everyone would immediately think she'll be interfering," explained Reg, "but, no, I went the other way and made her back him to the hilt. I hoped to bring out warmth in those attitudes."

The way that Helen has always interacted with the children, indeed with most of the characters in Ramsay Street at one time or another, casts her as the wise woman of the soap. She has helped almost everyone at some point.

She is a figure of authority — but also benign, understanding, sympathetic,

seasoned actors, Anne Haddy and Alan Dale.

Both have real-life experience of single parenthood. Anne brought up her children, Tony and Jane, for seven years on her own after her divorce. Alan brought up two sons after divorce from his wife.

And Anne is no stranger to life-threatening dramas. Heart disease, bypass surgery, stomach cancer and a broken hip have all featured as part of her own personal history. "I'm lucky to be alive," she says. "Life has become much more interesting to me, every minute of it."

Anne is a courageous woman, and her enthusiasm for life pervades the character of Helen. The sixty-year-old actress has survived all the set-backs in exactly the same manner we would expect Helen to respond.

"It's not hard proving Helen's real," she

"It's not hard proving Helen's real"

experienced, able to communicate with all the generations, diplomatic, intelligent, creative, sophisticated, the voice of calm and reason, and respected by all. No cardboard character this.

The screen presence of Helen, and the interplay between her and Jim, that other voice of calm strength in the neighbourhood, is the responsibility of two of the cast's most

says modestly, but then Anne Haddy has a lifetime of her own experiences with which to round and deepen the character. And wouldn't we all like someone like Helen in our lives to turn to when times get rough? Helen, the perfect granny, friend and mother-in-law, and still true to life — courtesy of Anne Haddy, classically trained actress.

> "A sermon in soaps . . . a celebration of the contemporary Australian way . . . high-grade comfort viewing."
>
> *Minette Marrin*
> *Daily Telegraph*

SOAP WARS

a game for 4 players, you need: 2 counters each
2 dice

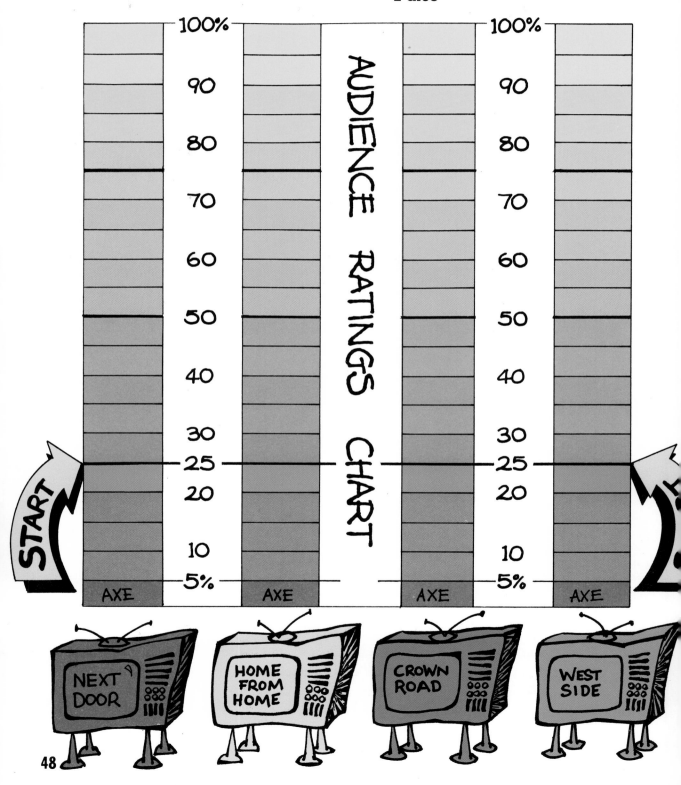

AUDIENCE RATINGS CHART

Now's your chance to run your own soap and chart your success in the audience ratings. Choose from one of the four soaps – NEXT DOOR, HOME FROM HOME, WESTSIDE, and CROWN ROAD. Each soap begins with 25% of the audience, an equal quarter share. You must survive star walkouts, rumours of splits in the cast, threats of axing, and thrive on the weddings, deaths and romances your storywriters can create.

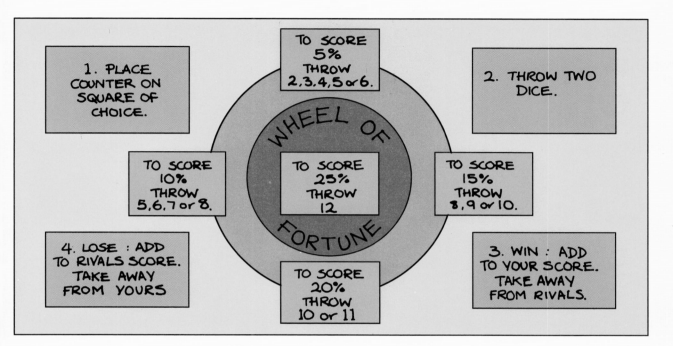

1. PLACE COUNTER ON SQUARE OF CHOICE.

TO SCORE 5% THROW 2,3,4,5 or 6.

2. THROW TWO DICE.

TO SCORE 10% THROW 5,6,7 or 8.

WHEEL OF FORTUNE

TO SCORE 25% THROW 12

TO SCORE 15% THROW 8,9 or 10.

4. LOSE : ADD TO RIVALS SCORE. TAKE AWAY FROM YOURS

TO SCORE 20% THROW 10 or 11

3. WIN : ADD TO YOUR SCORE. TAKE AWAY FROM RIVALS.

How to Play

Shake for who starts first. Place your counter on one of the squares on the wheel of fortune. Using two dice, if you can throw one of the numbers in the square you score the percentage increase shown. You add this to your score on the audience ratings chart, **and** take the same amount **away** from **one** of your rivals.

If you fail, however, you must take that percentage away from your score and add it to a rival's.

The Axe

If your soap falls to 5% on the ratings chart you must throw 5 or 6 to be allowed to continue in the game. If you fail you must go out of the game, and your 5% goes to the soap with the next lowest percentage rating.

Example

Your soap is NEXT DOOR. One of your counters marks your percentage on the ratings chart, let's say at 40%. Your nearest rival is CROWN ROAD on 35%. You place your other counter on 5% on the wheel of fortune, and throw a total of 6 with your two dice.

You win. Add 5% to your total (=45%), **and** take away 5% from CROWN ROAD (=30%). If you had lost you would have reduced your own score to 35%, **and** had to give 5% to one of your rivals.

The Winner

The winner is the first player to either reach an agreed percentage (say 80%), or to command more than 50% of the audience for 4 consecutive turns.

Now get in there and scrap it out. But remember, we want a good, clean fight – what else with soap?

SLIM AND SINGLE

Stefan Dennis *Paul*

There is no doubt that suave, slim Stefan Dennis, with the swept-back, black hair and big, brown eyes, fancies himself as a ladies' man. And since the exit of Jason and Craig from Neighbours he has had no trouble in assuming the mantle of the show's number one heart-throb. The only black cloud has been in real life.

Stefan is once more a single man. He and his stunning wife, Roz Roy, a model and TV game show presenter, parted quietly last year. Stefan blames the breakdown of his eleven-year marriage on his workload. He vigorously denies that the split was caused by either him or Roz finding a new partner.

"There were always two things in my life," he says. "Work and Roz. Things just got to the stage when the two didn't work alongside any more. With the time that we were spending on our careers it was just a gradual thing — we slowly drifted apart."

Stefan and Roz met when they were 16, and married at 21. "It's very difficult when you fall in love and get married when you're so young," says Stefan. "So many things happen, and you go through so many different experiences and changes that you come out of it completely different. To make

bellies, and I dread the day that I might get one, so I'm making sure I never will! I'm very conscious of my body, and look after it by working out and skipping every evening."

But that slim body and smooth looks landed him in trouble when he began globe-trotting to promote his launch into the pop world. He was photographed out on the town in London with Bananarama star, Jacqui Sullivan. The couple soon found themselves

"We slowly drifted apart"

a relationship work you have to spend a lot of time together and contribute as much as you can. I guess that I didn't do enough."

They may well have learned about life together, but in the course of that learning they found that in a lot of ways they were incredibly different. Simple things like shopping, for example. "Roz liked to buy whatever she wanted and ignore the price," says Stefan with a grimace. "She hated shopping with me because I'm a real bargain hunter and a serious-minded shopper. She couldn't handle that."

Certainly not when it came to cars. Stefan's nose for a bargain basement buy landed him a Porsche 911 Carrera. But at £55,000 it was obviously some new definition of bargain that Roz hadn't heard of. "I'm crazy about cars," admits Stefan, "but I'm not some sort of motoring playboy. And it's my only vice, and about all I spend money on."

fielding questions about a possible romance. "I'm not a marriage-wrecker," claimed Jacqui defiantly. "The reports are all nonsense."

It was all some paparazzi's pipe dream, claimed Stefan. The paparazzi had a lot more to say when Stefan's travels took him to a fun pub in Oldham, Lancashire. A young barmaid called Carol, a self-confessed **Neighbours** fan, had a very interesting story to tell. And tell all was precisely what she did, right across the headlines of a London newspaper. Worse still was her verdict on romantic Stefan. "For marks out of ten," said Carol, "I'll be kind and give him four."

Back on the **Neighbours** set Stefan was linked with his on-screen wife, Fiona Corke. "But there is nothing going on there," insists

"I'm crazy about cars"

Stefan does care a great deal about his looks as well. "I would hate to get fat more than anything else in the world," he confesses. "One of my pet hates is pot

Stefan. "We are just great friends. The whole cast is very close-knit. People seem to think I just click my fingers and girls come running. No way!"

But with looks like his who needs to click fingers?

"The characters are two-dimensional . . . [they are] so appalling you are horrified but hooked. They never change, whether they're blackmailed or shot by their wife."

Moira Petty
Today

MADGE AND HAROLD'S

A rainy January evening in Stockport, Cheshire would not be the first place you would think of looking for Ramsay Street regulars Madge and Harold Bishop. But last Christmas time that was exactly where you would have found actors Anne Charleston and Ian Smith. In panto.

Christmas pantomimes have become a home from home for the Aussie soap stars Peter O'Brien, Elaine Smith, Guy Pearce, Anne Charleston (twice) and Ian Smith, amongst others.

The land of fairytale suddenly has a distinctly Australian twang to its accent, but the entertainment and spectacle are as enjoyable as ever. The good guys still win, the bad boys get their comeuppance, the dame is outrageous and

the young lovers wander off to the sound of wedding bells at the end . . . not unlike the plot of a soap opera, except that this was delivered with songs, jokes and a little stage magic. Actors and audience alike drew great relish from the experience.

Thousands of fans bussed in from as far away as Scotland and Cornwall, and the sound of the **Neighbours** theme song sung by hundreds of youngsters was a prelude to every performance.

Dick Whittington drew record receipts of £500,000 at the Davenport Theatre, attracting 100,000 fans during its two month run. Amongst those seeing the show were cricket commentators Brian Johnson and Don Mosey, both avid fans. The production even drew the attention of millionaire John Paul Getty.

THE CARING TOUCH

Young or old, rich or poor, the British are in love with **Neighbours**. Both Anne and Ian repaid their fans not only with fine performances on stage, but also with the caring touch in the community.

A typical story is how the two popular Aussie stars helped young Erica Walsh. Erica had been in a coma since a road crash. Anne and Ian sent a

ADVENTURES IN ENGLAND

tape, urging Erica to get well and sending good wishes from the show.

Said her mum, Beryl, "It was just like a miracle. Everyone was around her bed and she started nodding and pointing and even took a cup off me to have a drink. That was the turning point. When she heard the tape she looked at her picture of Madge on the wall and to the television and started smiling. It was wonderful." Erica recovered enough to see the panto from a specially reserved front row seat, courtesy of Anne and Ian.

TV SCENES

While playing panto and making public appearances Anne and Ian also found time to film some scenes from forthcoming **Neighbours** episodes.

Beautiful Lyme Hall provided the backdrop for a storyline involving Harold's search for his ancestral roots, while Madge and he are on holiday in England. They bump into an eccentric aristocrat, Lord Ledgerwood, delightfully played by Derek Nimmo, whom they first mistake for the gardener. Well, he *is* shovelling stuff into a wheelbarrow, so it's a reasonable guess.

Derek Nimmo was delighted. "It was a great honour to be asked to appear in **Neighbours**. I've long been a fan of the show." But he was understandably disappointed that this didn't entail him jetting out to Melbourne for a few days in the sun during filming. (The BBC's *Holiday* programme paid him to do that instead!)

Britain has certainly turned out to be a lucky country for most of the **Neighbours** actors who have trodden these shores since the soap's rise to fame. And they'll be back. The Davenport Theatre in Stockport is continuing its run of **Neighbours** pantos, with its third in a row this Christmas, starring Rachel Friend and Craig McLachlan.

Last year, by the way, Harold was a rat. Oh yes he was!

Would you like to visit Daydream Island? You can – it's just off Shute Harbour in Queensland, one of many in Australia's extensive coastal waters. Australia is both the world's largest island and the smallest continent. Like satellites scattered along its north-eastern shores lie the emerald islands of the Great Barrier Reef.

This sprinkling of tropical paradises is no more than a boat ride away from the coast, and yet they provide everyone's idea of a faraway island . . . sun-drenched beaches and palm trees, the softness of the sand and the soothing breeze from the sea.

The Whitsunday Passage, through which you can hire a boat to sail, offers a staggering choice of 74 different islands. Everything from upbeat resorts to quiet backwaters is here.

The Islands

Photos by courtesy of the Australian Tourist Commission

AN ISLAND TO ESCAPE TO

Australia is rich in islands. One of them, Tasmania, is even big enough to be one of the Australian states. From the tropical heat of the north to the sub-Antarctic challenge to be found on the wild islands of the Bass Strait to the far south, Australia offers an island for everyone to escape to.

Islands to sail round. Islands to climb up and explore. Islands on which to unfold the pattern of flora and fauna. Islands on which to simply lie back and enjoy being exactly where you are.

WHERE LIVES THE QUOKKA

Many islands are home to wildlife: from the bird sanctuary on Michaelmas Cay off Cairns to Phillips Island off Victoria, home of the fairy penguin, there is variety everywhere. The misleadingly named Rottnest Island off Western Australia, where lives the quokka, a rare, small wallaby, has a curious history.

Early sailors thought the island to be covered in rats' nests. These were, in fact, nests belonging to none other than our little furry friends, the quokkas. And far to the south east of Rottnest lies Kangaroo Island, famous for sea-lions, pelicans, emus, Cape Barren geese, and, not surprisingly, kangaroos.

Fishing-diving-climbing-sailing-water-ski-ing-tennis-playing-windsurfing-horse-riding-swimming-caving-snorkelling-beachcombing-birdspotting-little Aussie islands. An island for everyone.

Craig McLachlan leaving **Neighbours** could have caused more than a few palpitations amongst his many fans, if it were not for the welcome news that he will still be on our screens, turning out for the opposition in *Home and Away* as teacher, Grant Mitchell. An improvement on Mr Fisher at least! Craig, well known for his appearances with and without clothes in **Neighbours** on Channel Ten in Australia, has already won back a sizeable chunk of audience for rival Channel 7. He made his debut in February this year, turning up to enter for Summer Bay's Mr Iron Man 1990.

Says Craig, "This bloke's not the flippant larrikin Henry was. He's got a handle on responsibility. He genuinely loves teaching and kids. There are some obvious, immediate differences in the character, so the actor side of me enjoys that."

Actress Danielle Carter rose to the considerable challenge of playing Jenny Owens with remarkable dedication. Jenny, a girlfriend of Mike's, is a paraplegic who is wheelchair-bound for life. Danielle found the six-week part very draining, both physically and emotionally. "It was exhausting trying to imagine and endure what these people have to go through," says Danielle, "and at the same time be a jolly soul, like so many paraplegics are. But I gave it my best shot. It was a good test." It's a pity that more popular TV shows don't acknowledge the fact that disabled people are part of everyday life, and no different from the rest of us.

If you feel hard done by at Britain lagging 18 months behind in screening **Neighbours** spare a thought for viewers in Perth. They are only six months ahead of us. Far worse is the fate that seems to have befallen viewers in Mackay, Queensland. After taking its customary Christmas break **Neighbours** simply failed to return. An anguished viewer rang local TV station MVQ6, only to be told that the programmers were having trouble 'finding a spot for it'. Instead, they're getting daily doses of a different soap, *Family Feud* (sounds a jolly show). Can you imagine what would happen if the BBC came up with the same excuse? The mind boggles!

Another contender for top Aussie soap is *Families*, and this time there was an absolute guarantee that British audiences would get to see the series from episode one at the same time as everyone else. The reason is that, in a bizarre but canny move, Granada Television moved their cameras Down Under to film this new £3 million soap series. It stars Australian comedian Barry Humphries' daughter, Tessa, and Scottish actor Malcolm Stoddard. The serial, which began shooting last March and opened in April, centres round a garage owner from Cheshire, in north-west England, who leaves his family to look for his first love in Sydney.

NEIGHBOURS NEWS

Lisa Armytage is a good actress, and she can say that with legal backing. Accepting undisclosed libel damages from The News Group Newspapers Limited, Lisa scotched stories that she had been sacked from **Neighbours** because of her poor acting ability. She claimed that it was the incompatibility of the exhausting schedule and her commitment to her young family that was the reason for her quitting. Indeed the producers tried very hard to persuade her to stay with the soap. Mr Justice Michael Davies believed her, and happy Lisa is now laughing all the way to the bank, her undoubted talents now recognized in a court of law.

New stars Jeremy Angerson (playing Josh Anderson) and Richard Norton (playing Ryan McLachlan) have scored a big hit in **Neighbours** Down Under. "My character's really good," says Jeremy. "He's a computer guy, and he does all these things like introducing computer viruses and upgrading people's marks! He's really good friends with Todd and Melissa."

Richard is equally enthusiastic about Ryan, who sounds not unlike Henry. "He's a surfie and he's very interested in girls. He's a natural sort of bloke, and he doesn't care what people think. He likes to plot and plan and rig things up. Ryan moves to Erinsborough when he gets kicked out of private school."

Arthur Scargill to star in **Neighbours**. Well, that might sound a trifle far-fetched, but trade unions in Australia have been approaching the top soaps to include stories about unions. Annie Jones has already lent her weight to just such a publicity campaign which boosted membership. A union official explained, "Soapies are very influential for teenagers and we'll be looking to promote the positive aspects of our work."

Paul Hogan

When Crocodile Dundee was released in 1986 it was an instant hit. It outgrossed *E.T.*, *Star Wars* and *Rambo*, all previous record-breaking blockbusters.

Paul Hogan had not always wanted to be an actor, though it seems he naturally had the comic touch. Born in 1939 in the tiny Outback settlement of Lightning Ridge, he grew up labouring, fighting and drinking.

He moved to Sydney and while a rigger on Sydney Harbour Bridge, he'd keep his mates amused with jokes and stories. In 1971, his mates persuaded him to have a go on Australian TV's talent show, *New Faces*.

Overnight millions of Australians were won over by his irreverent humour and deadpan delivery. He seemed so real, so funny, and so much one of them. Although he's called himself 'a Cinderella in hobnail boots' early success did not bring riches to match the fame; $40 a show was all he could command.

After two successful specials, made in Singapore and England, he began making *The Paul Hogan Show* in 1973. These introduced him to an international audience, and the late 1970s and 1980s brought superstardom. In fact Hogan – called Hoges by his mates – is, like the amber nectar he advertises, one of Australia's most successful exports.

Australian of the Year in 1986 for his services to tourism, he was also awarded membership of the *Order of Australia*. He's been honoured in the USA as well. April 30th 1986 was 'Paul Hogan Day' in Los Angeles!

Don Bradman

At less than 5'7" Don Bradman looked an unlikely hero, yet he is probably the greatest Australian cricketer on record. In his first class career he scored a century on better than one in every three appearances.

Altogether he made 117 first class centuries, including a highest score of 452 not out! As well as this record, he made six innings of over 300, and 37 of 200 or over.

Don's style was safety first. Unless his side was winning, he would always hit the ball along the ground. He was rarely caught, and was only run out four times in 338 first class innings.

From humble beginnings in Cootamundra, New South Wales, he rose to fame and international respect. In 1949 he became the first Australian knighted for his services to cricket.

Altogether he scored 6,996 runs in Test Matches, at an average of 99.94 an innings. His last Test Match appearance was against England in 1948, when he was bowled for a duck, sadly robbing him of a unique 100+ average. Few would forget, however, the genius of Bradman in his heyday, scoring 309 runs in a single day and thrilling crowds wherever he played.

He stands as a giant among Australians, and would perhaps have been mildly amused to know that he appeared in **Neighbours** – in the film Clive Gibbons showed at the Ramsay Farewell Party to mark Dan and Edna's divorce.

EXIT THE WICKED WITCH

Vivean Gray Mrs Mangel

When Nell Mangel and new husband, John Worthington, drove off into the sunset after the hiccups at their wedding, actress Vivean Gray, who played the wicked witch of Ramsay Street, was also driving out of the series.

Sadly, it was the fans who couldn't tell fact from fiction who helped her make up her mind to leave. Gentle, charming and softly spoken Vivean just could not take the abuse that followed her off screen. So convincing was her portrayal that some people could not believe she was only acting a part in **Neighbours**.

"We were disappointed," says script editor, Ray Kolle, "but not surprised when she said she was leaving. Kids would kick her in the street. Adults attacked her in the supermarket. It was terrible. I was stunned at the small-mindedness of an audience that couldn't distinguish between an actress and her on-screen character. The truth is that Vivean Gray couldn't be less like the wicked Mrs Mangel."

She found it very disturbing when irate fans invaded the garden of her modest suburban home in Melbourne. "It's very frightening," she says. "Playing such an unpleasant character can cause a lot of trouble. Some children even call me the local witch. I've had to call the police several times because of people tramping through my garden and banging on my door. I've had things said to me by children and teenagers that are so terrible I just couldn't repeat them."

Without the early morning calls to the Melbourne studios and script learning at the weekends, Vivean can also now afford to indulge in one of her favourite sports — watching cricket.

Clearly relishing her new-found freedom, Vivean continues, "Now I can start renewing old friendships, writing to my family in England, and doing a bit of photography, which I never had time to do." One thing is certain — there will be no more TV series for the veteran actress. "I'm getting to the age

"Children call me the local witch"

This is not a problem that likeable characters in soaps have to deal with. "In fact," Vivean adds, "it became so bad that I was afraid to go outside. I thought the best thing to do was leave the show. It was the only way to stop it."

Vivean took some time to make her decision to leave **Neighbours** after more than 600 performances. Admitting only to being 'around 60', she explains, "I'm at an age now when I could retire if I want to and it has crossed my mind. I've been in **Neighbours** for two and a half years and I've enjoyed every minute of it. But I'm afraid I've been rather typecast as a terrible woman in recent years and it has had a bad effect on me." Indeed, she had already played Mrs Jessup in *The Sullivans*, a busybody very much in the mould of Nell Mangel.

"I'm going to miss the cast of **Neighbours**. One of the plusses of working with all the cast was the friendly atmosphere when we were working. We worked hard but we had a heck of a lot of fun while we were doing it."

There are even fond memories of Nell Mangel too. "She was a wonderful character to play. She was like a catalyst sparking off confrontations between the other characters, and there was a lovely comedy element in the role."

Vivean also hopes she will rediscover her social life by turning her back on Ramsay Street. "Over the years," she says, "my social life has been shrinking and I know I'll be able to get it back and take up certain interests again."

where 7am calls are a bit much," she smiles. We may, however, see her again on screen in the odd, one-off drama . . . after her holiday.

"I'm just enjoying the rest and planning a lot of redecorating around my home, and a holiday somewhere off the beaten track, like desert India." Anywhere very remote, presumably, that hasn't yet heard of Mrs Mangel!

In the end Vivean has turned out to be her own worst enemy: Mrs Mangel was simply too real. Vivean Gray is too good an actress to give us anything less.

Meanwhile, the tradition of Mrs Mangel lives on in Ramsay Street. Sharp-tongued Hilary Robinson is the kind of relative most families are glad they only see on special occasions, if at all! Bubbly actress Anne Scott-Pendlebury took on the role of Jim's testy, spinster sister with relish.

"I adore Hilary," says Anne, "but I wouldn't have her for a friend. And I don't think I'd like her living below me because she would complain about my stereo."

Vivean Gray's experience was a lesson worth learning. "Hilary's an unpleasant character," says Anne. "I feel sorry for her. But I haven't had any hate mail which amazes me. I was warned that I might get unpleasantness on the street but that didn't worry me. I'm a lot younger than Hilary. I dress differently. In the street I go around in jeans."

Perhaps Anne has found the secret of being objectionable on screen and unrecognizable off. That's all to the good, for **Neighbours** producers say that the ghastly Hilary will be back!

ANSWERS

1. A motorbike
2. Perth
3. Mrs Mangel's
4. *Erinsborough News*
5. Fire damage
6. Wendy Gibson
7. Amanda lives in Hong Kong
8. Multiple sclerosis
9. Squawker
10. The son of Fred Mitchell and his girlfriend, Susan
11. She took the car keys from a drunken customer
12. Mrs Chubb
13. *I Believe*
14. Maths
15. At a dance
16. Hiccups
17. Tom, who owned Madge's house
18. Skinner, but Todd eventually beat him with a score of 70,500
19. Robbery
20. Alan Dale
21. S.J. Dey
22. Rev Sampson
23. Dentistry
24. Neddy
25. Tacky Tours
26. Anne Haddy
27. To become an airline steward
28. Mr Muir
29. The Y-Fronts
30. Sue Parker
31. It required Ramsay Street to be demolished
32. All methods used by Madge to stop Harold's snoring
33. Wilkins
34. Her memory
35. Her father, Dan
36. In a lift they were trapped in together
37. Henry
38. Paul's secretary
39. 18th March 1985
40. Scott
41. Anne Charleston and Ian Smith
42. Craig McLachlan
43. Alan Dale
44. The Ramsay and Gibbons Gardening Services
45. Dr Beverly Marshall
46. *Hot Cargo*
47. Her nephew
48. Four
49. The Robinsons
50. Blue

ANSWERS

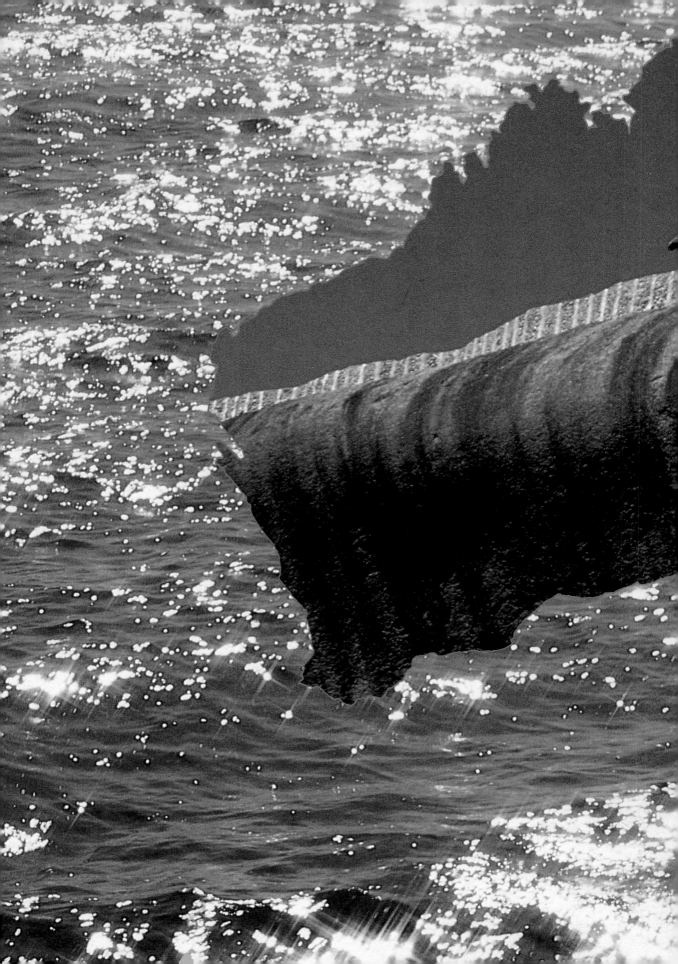